My Military Mommy and Military Daddy

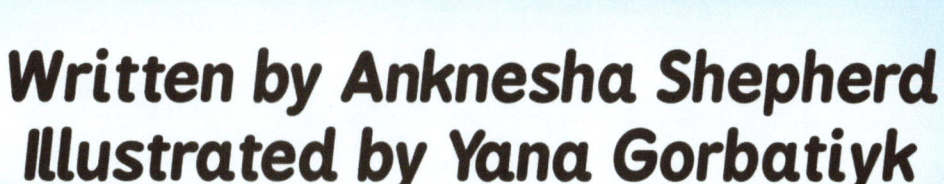

Written by Anknesha Shepherd
Illustrated by Yana Gorbatiyk

This book is for my son
and every military child
whose bedtime stories are sometimes read
over crackly phone calls or through tearful hugs.

May your dreams soar as high as the flags your
families defend.
You are strong, you are loved,
and your dreams matter.

With gratitude and hope —
for your sacrifices, your courage,
and the bright futures you're building
one dream at a time!

There is something special about my family.

My mommy and daddy are in the
military!

When you are a part of a military family things are a little different.

In the Military there is something called deployment. Deployment is when you are sent on a special assignment for the military

Luckily not at the same time, but it could happen.

When daddy leaves,
it's just mommy,
my sister,
and I.

This makes me sad at times. But I do talk to them on video calls and over the phone when they are gone.

But there is one amazing thing about mommy and daddy getting deployed.

They are then both back for a while, but then it's DUTY we have to worry about.

My daddy serves on a ship and my mommy is on shore duty!

So every few days it's just mommy, sister and I because daddy's on duty.

He has to sleep on the ship in a really small bed.

It is hard sometimes but we make it work.
Let's not even talk about before school and after school...

TAEKWONDO

Sometimes mommy has to drop me off at 6:30am, **can you believe it!**

School starts at 7:35am! But she has to make it work somehow.

I stay with the instructor and wait to go to school. But luckily, I am not the only military kid there! There are lots of us!

We play together before school starts,
how cool is that!

After school, we get to play again because mommy and daddy have to work late!

Even though we have to be apart at times, it makes the time spent together even better.

I love my military parents!

MY Military Mommy & Military Daddy

ankoredcreations@gmail.com

title: **My Military Mommy and Military Daddy/ Anknesha Shepherd**

Identifiers: **ISBN: 979-8-9927348-0-5 (paperback)**

Any references to historical events, real people, or real places are used fictitiously. Names, characters, and places are products of the author's imagination.

Published and Printed in the USA

First Printing Edition **2025**.
Publisher: **Chick Chief Publishing**

www.ingramcontent.com/pod-product-compliance
Lightning Source LLC
Chambersburg PA
CBHW041604120626
46551CB00002B/302